Contents

Football fans singing.
People in a crowd often break
into song when they are happy.

Why sing and dance?

Why do we sing? Why do we play music and dance?
People have music and dancing all over the world.
Singing and dancing seem to be born in us.
They are an instinct. They come naturally.

Many animals also have this instinct.
Birds sing. They often dance too.
They do this to attract a mate in the spring.
Or they dance to warn off an enemy.

Animals have love dances. They have war dances too.
Sometimes their play is a kind of dancing.

These are impala.
They are light on their feet
and jump very high.
These are playing
a fighting game.
They do it like a dance
and do not hurt each other.

Music
and
Dancing

Action World

Macdonald Educational

First published in Great Britain 1977
by Macdonald Educational Ltd
Holywell House, Worship Street
London EC2A 2EN

ISBN 0 356 05565 5

Planned and edited by Dale Gunthorp
Text by M. L. McCarthy
Consultants: Jean Cooper
and Lila Horne

Cover: Hayward Art Group

Photographic sources: British
Museum 12; British Tourist Authority
18, 29; CBS 41B; Central Press 19T;
Coloursport 4–5; Epic 39; Fotomas
Index 13, 26; Galerie der Staat 33;
Kunsthistorische Museum, Vienna
13T; Robert Harding 15T; Alan
Hutchinson 30; Island 41T; Kobal
Collection 38; Macdonald (Dennis
Moore) 7B, 8T, 17B, 16, 28B, 45T;
Mander and Mitchenson Theatre
Collection 36; Motown 40; National
Gallery 22; Neumeister 23B; Popper
39; Royal Opera House and
Woodmansterne 23T; SEF 15B, 28T;
Starr-Duffy 20; Robert Stigwood
Group 37; Valerie Wilmer 31T, 31B;
ZEFA 9T, 14.

Printed by Morrison & Gibb Ltd,
London and Edinburgh.

We first learn singing and dancing
from people round us.
Tiny children copy the songs and steps.
Older children, or parents, show them how.

We first learn easy steps and short songs.
Mothers may sing to their babies.
Mothers all over the world do this.
The baby is happy when its mother sings.

▲

This man is an Aborigine
from Australia.
He is doing a tribal dance.

►

This little girl
has picked up dance steps
from other people.
Some children's games
have dances in them.
Ring-o-roses and
oranges and lemons
are dancing games.
Can you think of others?

All over the world

There is music and dancing all over the world.
Some lands have music
which sounds odd to us.

Eastern music is not like Western music.
We find Eastern music hard to understand.
We often like the sound of Indian music.
But we find it hard to follow the tune.
Japanese music is even more different.
Some people think it is all clanks and bangs.
They do not understand it at all.

Yet we often like music from Africa.
Our popular music often has an African beat.
So we can understand some African music.

These boys are tapping out
drum rhythms.
They are playing
West African music.
You might find their
rhythms hard to play,
but you would understand
the beat.

Classical music
comes from Europe.
It was written for kings
and rich people.
Now we have concerts
and records
and everyone can
listen to it.
This is a small concert
in Russia.

These dancers
are Indians from Mexico.
They are doing an old
Aztec dance.
The movements are slow
and graceful.
These dances were danced
for gods and kings
long ago.

9

The beginnings

People think dancing came before music.
The first dancers made their own rhythm.
They stamped their feet on the ground.
Later they may have banged sticks.
This would be the start of drumming.

Then people began to make music
with instruments.
Long ago in Egypt they played drums.
They had flutes and lyres too.
The dances may have been rather like ballet.

This picture is thousands of years old.
It shows how people danced
and played music
in the Middle East long ago.

The first musicians
played drums.
They sang or chanted songs.
This was mostly
music of rhythm.
It had very few notes.

Later came flutes and harps.
Blowing instruments
such as flutes
make more tunes.

Harps and other instruments
are played with strings.
They are good for rhythm
as well as the tune.

The tune of music
is called the melody.

These instruments
come from West Africa.
They are different from
instruments you may know.
But they work
in the same way.
People have used instruments
like these
for thousands of years.

This rhythm
instrument is
called a
balafon.

This pipe is
a shepherd boy's
flute.

The men are playing
bow-harps.
The boy is playing
a hand drum.

11

Nobles and peasants

There are two kinds of music and dance.
One is people's music and dancing. This is folk music.
It is song and dance for everybody.

The other music and dance is for great events.
This is much harder to do.
People train for years to learn it.
They also need a natural gift.

Long ago kings and nobles hired musicians.
Dancers also danced for them.
This was the start of opera and ballet.
Classical music also began in this way.
Classical music was music of the court.
Folk music was music of the common people.

Musicians of the Middle Ages.
These men played for nobles.
They played the first
court music of Europe.

▲ This painting shows how peasants danced in Europe 400 years ago. Their dances were wilder and more free than court dances.

▼ The minuet was a court dance. Dancers wore tight shoes and clothes. The dance was slow and graceful.

Religion

Simple people lived a life full of dangers.
The crops might fail. Babies might die. Enemies might make war.
They sang and danced to their gods.
They asked the gods for help.
Music and dancing became part of religion.

Churches all over the world have music.
Many churches have dancing too.
Music and dance lift our spirits.
They take away the cares of daily life.
They can make us think about religion.

These children are singing
in a Catholic church at Easter.

These Indians from Mexico are dancing for their gods.

Islam has less music and dance than other great religions.

But in Africa Islam has more music.

These drummers are playing at a religious festival.

High days and holidays

Big holidays and carnivals are often great days.
There will be music and dancing.
People often sing and dance
when they are happy in a crowd.
It does not matter, then,
who is rich and who is poor.
All the people belong together.
For a time, everyone loves his neighbour.

Rio, in Brazil, has a famous carnival.
People dress up and go into the streets.
The party lasts for a few days.

Dancers at the Rio carnival.
This is the time when all Rio
lets its hair down.

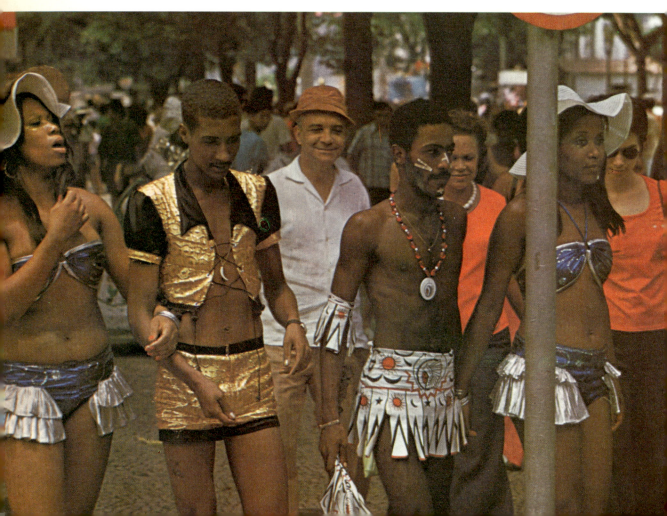

These girls are taking part
in a display at a school
in Canada.

They are marching to music
of a brass band.

These displays are held
on special school holidays.

In some parts of Africa
each town has its own festival.
Some have dances for men
or women only.
This is a women's dance
in West Africa.

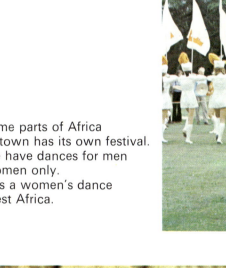

War

Some war songs and dances are very old.
Music and dancing can make people
feel strong and brave.
A war dance can help men get ready to fight.
People also danced war dances to ask their gods
to help them win. Tribes still do these dances.

Modern wars are fought with machines.
There is no place for the bold dance before battle.
But soldiers still sing.
They sing to keep their spirits up on long marches.
They sing and dance to stop them feeling home-sick.
Every war has its soldiers' songs.
'Tipperary' and 'Lily Marlene' are soldiers' songs.
They come from the two world wars.

The Guards' bands, in London.
Brass band music is played
by soldiers all over the West.
The music is exciting
and has a good beat
for marching.

Dancing in the streets, London, 1918.
The First World War was over.
People danced for joy.

Bob Dylan singing anti-war songs.
War music is bold and full of fire.
Anti-war music also touches people's feelings.
But it does this by making people think
of all the killing and grabbing of war.

Ballet

The most famous
of the dances of Europe
is the ballet.

Ballet tells a story
set to music.
The dancers use movement
and mime
instead of words.
They wear costumes
and the stage has scenery.

Dancers train for years
to learn ballet.
They have to be very fit
and very strong.
Yet they seem light as birds
when they dance.

In classical ballet
all the steps are
worked out first.
The dancers learn
their steps by heart.
In modern ballet
the dancers make up
some of their steps
as they dance.

Ballet started in France
about 400 years ago.
Ballet steps still have
French names.

These dancers make ballet look easy.
It isn't!
The woman is balanced on the tip of her toe.
She makes this look quite natural
because she does it with grace.
This movement is called an 'arabesque'. ▼

Ballet dancers use mime
as well as dance.
Mime tells a story
without words.
This ballerina is dancing
the part of a mad girl.
See her face and hands.
They show how sad
and worried she is.

Opera and concert

These three musicians
are giving a concert.
They are singing
and one plays a lute.
This picture was painted
before the time of big concerts.
Concerts became important
in the time classical music
was first written, 300 years ago.

An opera is a play
set to music.
The story may be funny.
Or it may be sad.
Many operas have dancing
as well as music.

The words of the opera
are called the libretto.
In grand opera
the story is often
about love and murder.

There are songs
called arias.
Some arias from opera
have become popular songs.

Concerts began when people
sat down to listen
to music played by itself.
At the first concerts
friends came to a house
to hear a musician play.
Later big concerts
were held
in halls and palaces.

Then classical music
became very important.
It developed fast.
Concerts made people listen
very closely to music.

▲

This scene comes from
'Lucia di Lammermore'.
Lucia faints when her lover
tells the men to kill him.
He thinks Lucia wants to be free
to marry another man.

This opera has a story
full of madness and killing.
Grand opera often does.

This group of four musicians
is called a quartet.
They play a viola, a cello
and two violins.
They are the Amadeus Quartet.
They give many concerts.

Orchestra

A group of musicians
may play together.
This is an orchestra.
A band is a small orchestra.

Big orchestras today
have about 100 players.
A conductor keeps them
all in order.
He beats time with a stick.
This is called a baton.
He tells the players
when to begin.
He tells them when to play
loudly or softly.

Big orchestras play
for opera and ballet.
They also play symphonies
and other concert music.

1

2

3

1. The strings. The string section
of the orchestra has violins, violas
cellos and double bass.
The lute (shown here) and guitar
are other important string instruments.

2. The percussion. This part
of the orchestra has rhythm instruments
like the kettle-drums.

3. Wind. Instruments you blow into
are called wind instruments. This man is
playing a flute. Other wind instruments,
such as the trumpet, are called the 'brass'.

An orchestra playing in the Opera House,
Sydney, Australia.
The musicians sit in a half-circle
round the conductor. ▶

25

Writing it all down

1,400 years ago people began to write down music. They wanted to remember chants they sang in church. At first they just had curves. These showed how the tune went up or down.

Later they had square notes on paper with lines. Each note stood for a sound.

Now we have round notes. We write them on five lines. The notes are on the lines or between them. Different notes are used for long or short sounds.

Some people can read music. They can sing a song from the written music. This is easy for them. They can read notes just as you read words.

▲ People used to write square notes like this.

► Modern music has round notes.

The five basic positions of ballet

It is more difficult to write
dance than to write music.
There are two ways to write
ballet.
Both are very hard to follow.

But the basic movements
of ballet are well known.
They were made up by dancers
in France 300 years ago.

These dancers made up
five basic positions,
and seven basic movements.
These pictures show
the five basic positions.

Every dance in classical
ballet begins and ends
with one of these positions.

Position 1

Position 2

Position 3

Position 4

Position 5

Folk song and dance

These two pictures show song and dance from Russia. The people wear folk costume.

28

Many lands have a national costume.
People often wear it to do their folk dances.
They wear it to play and sing folk music.

Folk music is often very old.
There are old dances to welcome the spring.
They were once part of very old religions.
England still has Morris dancing from pagan times.

Many old songs and dances have been lost and forgotten.
This is happening in Africa and Asia now.
Country people go to live in towns.
They forget their old folk ways.
But some folk music and dancing is being saved.
People are writing down the old songs and dances.

Morris dancers.
Long ago the men had
green branches instead
of streamers.

▼

Poor folk

One kind of folk music means a great deal to us.
This is the music made by slaves in America.
These slaves were taken from Africa.
They lost their homes and families. They lost their languages.
But they kept some African music and dance.

In America the slaves became Christians. They learnt hymns.
They made a new music. It had African rhythm.
But some tunes came from hymns.
The songs were often very sad.
These were the famous negro spirituals.

Modern music has learnt new rhythm
and spirit from the slaves' music.

In Africa many people sing while they work.
The rhythm helps them keep going
when work is hard or dull.

▲
A funeral in New Orleans, America.
This wild dance helps to take away
some of the sadness.
And it gives the dead person a
send-off into the promised land.

Gospel singers in church ▶
in the American South.
Their music comes from some
of the songs sung by slaves.
Gospel music is the church music
of black America.

Jazz

Jazz started in the United States around 1900.
It grew out of spirituals, blues and ragtime.
Jazz was invented by black Americans.
But white musicians have always played it too.

Jazz has a strong rhythm,
so at first people liked to dance to it.
After about 1940, modern jazz grew up.
People sat and listened to it
because it was a more serious kind of music.

Most jazz players can read music.
But they mainly improvise their music.
This means that they make up new tunes
as they go along, without reading music.
These new tunes are called solos.
Each musician takes his turn to play a solo.

 ▲

Many people think
that Bessie Smith
was the greatest
blues singer.

◄

Jelly Roll Morton
(at the piano)
said he made jazz happen.
In fact he was not the
only one playing jazz.

►

Jazz caught on in the West
after the First World War.
Jazz bands played at dances.
People loved its rhythm,
and the 1920s were called
'The Jazz Age'.

Ballroom

Long ago the King of France loved dancing.
He held great balls at his palace.
People put on their best clothes.
They danced minuets and other courtly dances.
People had a chance to show off their jewels.
Young people looked for someone to marry.
Everybody was very polite.

Ballroom dancing was very popular
after the First World War.
There were many dances to learn.
There was the waltz, the quick-step, the fox-trot.
People had lessons in ballroom dancing.
Ballroom dancing competitions are still popular.

'The Lambeth Walk' was
a ballroom dance with
a music hall rhythm.
Everyone danced it for
a while, then forgot it.

Other dance fads were the
tango, veleta, cha-cha-cha,
mambo, rumba,
and many others.

A ballroom in the 1900s.
Girls sat in lines around the room.
Men would ask them to dance.
Girls were never allowed
to make the first move.
This was one of the rules of ballroom.

Dancing in the fox-trot
in the 1920s.
This was worlds away
from the jazz clubs.

Some dances were fast. Some had tricky foot-work.
Most ballroom dances had strict rules.
They were dances for 'ladies' and 'gentlemen'.

But life was changing. Jazz came into the ballroom.
Jazz rhythms were too hot for the old dances.
People wanted their dancing to be a little wild.
Jitterbug, then jive, became more popular than ballroom.

Music hall and musical

Music hall was a show on stage. It had songs, dances and jokes.
It began in England about 1840.
It was very popular until the time of films.
Music hall was called vaudeville in America and France.

Leading men and women sang the big songs.
A chorus of girls danced between the songs.
A 'Master of Ceremonies' kept things moving.
Many acts and songs poked fun at important people.

Many popular songs of the early 20th century
came from music hall.
All people, rich and poor, picked up music hall songs.
Poor people sang the songs in pubs,
or they sang them while they worked.

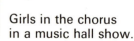

Girls in the chorus
in a music hall show.

Judas and a chorus of angels
from 'Jesus Christ Superstar'.
This musical has rock music.

Musicals started in America.
They are also shows with music and dancing.
But they are more like opera. They tell a story.
The first big musical was 'Showboat'.
Then came 'Oklahoma!'.
Many musicals were made into films.

Musicals are very expensive to make.
They have big casts. They need costumes, scenery.
On stage they need long runs to make any money.
But on film they can earn a fortune.

Pop and rock

Rock'n'roll took the world by storm in the 1950s.
Chuck Berry, Bill Haley and Elvis Presley played a simple form of blues.
They used electric guitars and a thumping beat.
Rock was rough, loud and simple.
Teenagers found it wild and exciting. But their parents and teachers hated it.

Pop music changed with the Beatles, 10 years later.
The Beatles took ideas from the folk music of the 1960s.
They used their songs to try to make sense of the world.
Then many older people also began to like pop music.
Then came the Rolling Stones.
Their music was wild and angry.

Elvis Presley in 'Jailhouse Rock'.
Elvis had a 'tough' image.
He was one of the first rock stars.

◄ The Beatles
came from Liverpool
and shot to world fame.

Abba, the group
from Sweden.
▼ They sing songs rather
like the Beatles.

Reggae, soul and country

Soul is one kind of black music from America.
It has its roots in negro spirituals and the blues.
It comes from Gospel music.
Soul is played with modern electric instruments.
It is music full of deep and strong feeling.

Reggae is also played with electric instruments.
It comes from poor parts of Jamaica.
It is linked with the Rastafarian religion.
It is a form of rock. It has become very popular.

Country and Western music also comes from America.
It comes from the songs of poor white farm people.
It grew out of cowboy songs and folk songs of Europe.

Stevie Wonder,
the blind
▼ soul singer
of Motown.

Bob Marley and the Wailers,
a Reggae group.
Reggae is good dance music.

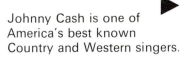
Johnny Cash is one of
America's best known
Country and Western singers.

New technology

Rock groups today spend thousands on gear.
Most big groups have three electric guitars.
There are lead, rhythm and bass guitars.
Groups have a drum kit with bass drum, snare drum,
and tom-toms. They also have cymbals.

And they have amplifiers, mikes and mixers.
Some have an electric piano or organ.
Some have a synthesiser.
This makes sound by electronics.

A rock musician
with some of the group's gear.
Now it costs thousands
to get a group together.
Elvis just started with a guitar!

Broadcasting music also needs
very costly technology.
Here a disc jockey is at work.

▼

All the people

People need to sing, play music and dance.
Music makes us feel glad and alive.
It takes away our loneliness.
It makes us part of a group.
Football fans singing at a game feel
as if the whole crowd has moved into the clouds.
So do opera singers, or violin players.
So do people dancing at a carnival.

People are always making up new songs and dances.
The world is always changing. We change too.
New music, new dances, show us our new selves.

These children are moving
to rhythm.
This is a simple form
of dancing.
They are moving to show
how they feel.

▲
These musicians
are playing
for all the people
passing by.

People at a ▶
pop concert.
They are listening
to a new group.
If they like the group
they can make it
famous.

Index

Figures in **heavy** type
show the pictures.